The New Global Currency: REAL ESTATE

INVESTMENT

REAL ESTATE IS THE NEW GLOBAL CURRENCY

As equity markets get routed worldwide, there is a flight to real estate.

Markets are crashing all over. It started with the Greece turmoil, China market taking a rout and then the US market taking a breather. So the question in most investors' mind is: "Where to park funds in these turbulent times in order to have peace of mind rather than having sleepless nights?" The answer is: Real estate which is emerging as the new global currency.

The unthinkable had just happened - the people of Greece had voted to tell the big European banks and their political lapdogs to go pound sand. This proves the axiom by John Paul Getty: "If you owe the bank USD100, that's your problem. If you owe the bank USD100 million, that's the bank's problem."

Latest from Bloomberg:

China's Shanghai Composite Index plunged amid concern a raft of measures to stabilise equities is failing to stop the bear-market rout as traders unwind margin bets at a record pace. The Shanghai Composite tumbled as much as 8.2 per cent, the most since 2007, before paring losses to 4.8 per cent to trade at 3,549.92 at 9:56 am local time. There were four gainers among the 1,106 stocks that trade on the benchmark gauge, which has slumped 28 per cent since the June peak. PetroChina Co., the biggest stock, tumbled 4.9 per cent as nine out of 10 industry gauges dropped at least 4 per cent in the CSI 300 Index.

Plunging Chinese equities have damaged the confidence of its main driving force -- the more than 90 million individual investors who make up about 80 per cent of the market, according to a survey of households.

The recent events in Europe, China and the Middle East clearly demonstrate that clients are now pulling their funds out of the equity market which is turning into an asset bubble and can collapse any time. There is strong correlation between equity bubbles and upsurge in real estate globally. This is the best opportunity for savvy investors to take a long position in real estate for their wealth preservation. Real estate has become the new safe haven for smart investors globally.

So, people in Greece, Italy, France and Spain are getting their funds out of the banks and buying properties in Kuala Lumpur, London, Dubai, Melbourne, Istanbul and New York. Rich Chinese, European and American investors are investing in trophy investment assets in residential and commercial properties.

The growing wealth in Asia provides plenty of opportunities for the clients to have their wealth protected as markets get more edgy and uncertain. ■

Shan Saeed is Chief Economist and Investment Strategist at IQI Group Holdings, a property and investment company operating and advising clients in Kuala Lumpur, Singapore, Hong Kong, London, Melbourne and Dubai.

"Reproduced with permission from Asian Property Review"

The New Global Currency: REAL ESTATE

How to Invest like Savvy Investors
and to Stay Ahead of the Market
in these Turbulent Times

DANIEL HO;SHAN SAEED;KASHIF ANSARI

PARTRIDGE
A Penguin Random House Company

Print information available on the last page.

To order additional copies of this book, contact
Toll Free 800 101 2657 (Singapore)
Toll Free 1 800 81 7340 (Malaysia)
orders.singapore@partridgepublishing.com

www.partridgepublishing.com/singapore

FOREWORD

There is a time and a place for everything and now is the time for real estate in the ASEAN region. Cash can be printed without control and devalued overnight; other asset classes such as stocks, precious metals, commodities do fluctuate and have dipped in price at times. So what do the savvy investors and the wealthy people do? They choose an asset class that has shown time and time again tko provide steady gains. And given the right time and right place, the gains can be very substantial. They are putting their money in real estate and ASEAN is the growth story of the decade.

This book will analyze the trend and reasoning behind the shift of wealth holding to real estate, as well as zoom in on ASEAN and countries within the region to identify the biggest potential areas and how to capitalize on them. Key strategies and criteria will be revealed in simple yet applicable ways that readers will be able to start investing like savvy investors in no time. Specific investment regions and areas will be discussed in the following Topics as part of the analysis of the ASEAN region and further zooming in on certain countries and specific hot spots with great potential.

The authors are savvy investors who also serve as advisors to high net worth individuals and corporations who want to preserve and grow their wealth in the most strategic and profitable manner.

ABOUT DANIEL HO

Daniel Ho is the Group Managing Director of IQI. He speaks and lectures regularly at various companies and universities on the topic in personal development and investments. Daniel is responsible for the organisational long term growth, development projects, strategic alliances and he also heads the group marketing division and oversees the IQI Wealth Hub.

Daniel has over 20 years of experience in the Malaysian corporate and business market and brings with him expertise in strategy, operations, fund raising and investments having worked for many leading MNCs and Malaysian firms.

Daniel was actively involved in the Malaysia Real Estate sector and was managing large property funds for high net worth clients.

ABOUT SHAN SAEED

Shan Saeed is Chief Economist / Investment Strategist at IQI Group Holdings, a leading property and investment company operating and advising clients in Kuala Lumpur, Singapore, Hong Kong, London, Melbourne and Dubai. He has 15 years of solid financial market experience in the areas of private banking, risk /compliance management, commodity investments, global economy and business strategy.

He has been quoted on Bloomberg, Al Jazeera TV, Hubbis Hong Kong, CNBC Singapore, Channel News Asia Singapore, International New York Times, FT [Deutschland], Italian wealth management magazine, Islamic Finance News Malaysia, Smart Investor, Money Compass, Rotary Club USA, World Business Journal Singapore, Focus Malaysia, Oil/Gas magazine Malaysia, Business Today and many more. Shan blogs at www.economistshan.blogspot.com

He has graduated from one of the top elite business schools in USA i.e. Booth School of Business at the University of Chicago [USA]. He got his first MBA from IBA Pakistan [in collaboration with the Wharton School, University of Pennsylvania]. He is also trained in Alternative Banking/ Strategies from the Harvard Business School, USA

ABOUT KASHIF ANSARI

Kashif Ansari is the Group CEO at IQI. He oversees all investments activities and is responsible for global investor relationships, deal origination, corporate fund raising and business development for the group.

Kashif has over 20 years of experience in the field of investment management, corporate finance, private equity, principal financing, real estate investment and strategy. His experience covers both emerging and developed markets including the Asia Pacific, MENA region, the United States and Europe.

Kashif has a bachelors in Accounting and an MBA with concentrations in Finance, Entrepreneurship & Innovation and Management & Strategy.

Daniel's Dedication

I wish to dedicate this book to my family, friends, and various mentors who have supported me in my life journey and for helping me to be where I am today.

I also want to dedicate this to my partners in IQI Holdings who have worked closely together to build businesses in a fun and friendly way.

And lastly, to my co-authors who have committed to their time and effort to produce this book with the intention of sharing this knowledge with the world.

My sincere love and appreciation to all of you!

Shan's Dedication

I dedicate this book to my late father SAEED HAFEEZ who supported my winning moments to give up his moments. My beautiful mother AFTAB SAEED who is always praying for me and my family.

I dedicate to my Nobel Laureate professors from University of Chicago, Booth School of Business, USA: Prof. Gary Becker [Late], Prof. Milton Friedman [Late], Prof. Robert Fogel [Late], Prof. Eugene Fama, Prof. John Huizinga.

My professors from Institute of Business Administration, Karachi, Pakistan: Feisal Rahimtoola, Syed Fazle Hassan [Late], Dr. Mehnaz Fatima, Dr. Hafiz Pasha, Dr. Abdul Wahab.

All my teachers at Brooklyn school / St. Pauls High School and D.J. Science College; my partners and colleagues at IQI: Mr. Abdul Rahman Dakri, Kashif Ansari, Daniel Ho, Sheila Tan, Nabeel Mungaye, Shahid Saleem, Kelvin Hoe, Anthony Lim, Alexander Woo.

To my Malaysian and global friends: SPAD Chairman-Tan Seri Dato Sr Syed Hamid Albar, Famous lawyer Puan Sri Devi, Dato Ghazali, Dato Zaha Rina, Tan Sri Dr Michael Yeoh, Dato Iqbal, Dato Hamza, Woon Teck Seng, Tan Sri P Alagendra, Sophie Kamruddin and Azreen from Bloomberg, Melissa Goh--Bureau Chief Channel News Asia KL, Sheung Un--BFM89.9, Peter Yang, Peter Lim, Yuki Aizawa, Cherie Siew Ling Wong, Flaminia Lilli, Max Shangkar, Dato Danny, Tan Sri Tajuddin, Tan Sri Jeffrey Cheah, Jim Rogers, Shaun Rein, Sameer Chishty, Saeed Chinoy, Arif Lateef, Philips Singlekow, Michael Stanhope, Eva Law, Libby Gill and Angel Ann; my sincere friends / well wishers all over the globe in 157 countries. Dedicated to all. Thank you.

Kashif's Dedication

To my parents Mahmood and Nasima, who walked me to school and took me to the library!

To my wife Heba, without whose support, care and patience this would not have been possible.

To my two beautiful daughters, Hasna and Zainab, who are the pearls in my life.

To my brothers Noman and Salman,, and sister Shazia - thank you for sharing your company, humor, pain and joy.

To my team at IQI, especially Mr. Dakri, Daniel Ho, Sheila Tan, Kelvin Hoe, Shan Saeed, Nabeel Mungaye, Shahid Saleem, Anthony Lim and Moazzam Ali – thank you for your support.

To the mentors in my life who have equipped me with knowledge and experience, Tan Sri Dato' Mohamed Mansor Bin Fateh Din, Ishaque Noor, Zafar Ahmad, Scott Mandell and Joel Warady.

To my friends and people who have made a difference in my life, Jamal Salem, Dr Mahmood Ahmad, Shahram Bakhtiari, Sajjid Sadiq, Mudassir Amray, Tanweer Bukhari, Yahya Ismail, Rafique Lakhani, Fatimah Abd Wahab, Junaid Zikar, Arif Latif, Amin Khan, Datuk N.K. Tong, Chris Tan, Shahid Malik, Faraz Malik, Adil Rasheed, Yusuf Pingar, Azam Zaka and Aftab Khan.

To all the above who have shown me how to DREAM BIG and ENJOY LIFE!

TABLE OF CONTENTS

Topic 1

Global Economic Outlook

This topic explores some of the largest and most influential economies in today's world. Some of them have had a good run for years or decades and that run might be coming to an end. It is not just about economic cycles or predictions but rather on hard facts on a country's fundamental economic factors. Once that is out of place, no country can sustain a healthy economic outlook.

Scary Outlook of the US Economy

The United States could soon become a large-scale Spain or Greece, teetering on the edge
of financial ruin. That's according to Donald Trump, who painted a very ugly picture of where this country is headed. Trump made the comments during a recent appearance on Fox News' "On the Record with Greta Van Susteren". According to Trump, the United States is no longer a rich country. "When you're not rich, you have to go out and borrow money. We're borrowing from the Chinese and others. We're up to $16 trillion in debt."
He goes on to point out that the downgrade of US debt is inevitable.

Savvy investors are taking steps to protect their wealth and that is exactly what many well-respected economists, billionaires, and noted authors are advocating. Experts such as Marc Faber, Peter Schiff, Donald Trump, and Robert Wiedemer are saying that the US is on the verge of another recession, and this one will be far worse than what she experienced during the last financial crisis.

Marc Faber, the noted Swiss economist and investor, has voiced his concerns for the U.S. economy numerous times during recent media appearances, stating, "I think somewhere down the line we will have a massive wealth destruction. I would say that well-to-do people may lose up to 50 percent of their total wealth."

The chart, recently republished by Mark Hulbert on MarketWatch, shows a direct correlation between today's stock market and the one leading up to the historic 1929 collapse.

The shocking parallel confirms what some experts say is in store for the US economy in 2014 and 2015: a stock market crash by about 50 to 70%. The recent injection of funds into the US market by its government has kept the outlook artificially positive for the time being but anyone with common sense knows that this is not a sustainable model. It is all artificially inflated by the Federal Reserve of US it is a matter of time before it all falls apart.

Market Players Insight: Pulling Out Of Equity Assets

A handful of billionaires are quietly dumping their American stocks . . . and fast. Warren Buffett, who has been a cheerleader for US stocks for quite some time, is dumping shares at an alarming rate. He recently complained of "disappointing performance" in dyed-in-the-wool American companies like Johnson & Johnson, Procter & Gamble, and Kraft Foods.

Buffett's holding company, Berkshire Hathaway, has been drastically reducing his exposure to stocks that depend on consumer purchasing habits. Berkshire sold roughly 19 million shares of Johnson & Johnson, and reduced its overall stake in "consumer product stocks" by 21%. Berkshire Hathaway also sold its entire stake in California-based computer parts supplier Intel.

With 70% of the U.S. economy dependent on consumer spending, Buffett's apparent lack of faith in these companies' future prospects is worrisome. Unfortunately Buffett isn't alone.

Policy Uncertainty in US and Europe

Policy uncertainty makes a huge impact and is hurting the economies. Even when the fundamentals of an economy are right, there can only be growth when there is public confidence in the government and in the economy. A lack of confidence would result in holding back of spending and investing for the reason of keeping reserves for a rainy day. And an uncertainty in policy makes it difficult to predict what will happen next and thus causes uncertainty or low confidence in the public.

Some of the following are consequences of policy uncertainty:

Area of Uncertainty	Result of Uncertainty
Investment	Decreases both private and public
Consumption	Lowers domestic demand leading to recession
CAPEX	Difficult to execute for big projects
Economic signals	Bad for the market sentiments and players

Taxes in the USA have Increased

It was reported by Ziad Abdelnour, President and CEO of Blackhawk Partners, Inc USA, that as of 1st January 2014 certain taxes have been amended and that these taxes were all passed only with democrat votes, no republicans voted for these taxes. These taxes were all passed under the Affordable Care Act, a.k.a. Obamacare.

Tax Category	Previous Rate (%)	New Rate (%)	Increase (%)
Top Medicare tax	1.45	2.35	0.9
Top Income tax bracket	35.0	39.6	4.6
Top Income Payroll tax	37.4	52.2	14.8
Capital Gains tax	15.0	28.0	13.0
Dividends tax	15.9	39.6	23.7
Estate tax	0.0	55.0	55.0

There have been some significant increase in tax and this is not a good sign. The USA has been pumping in cash to stimulate the economy and it is no surprise that they need to replenish their funds. Tax is one way to do it and thus it is an indicator that the government is running short of funds. It is already well known that the USA has huge debts; increasing taxes will ease the government's cash flow but will decrease the people's spending power, effectively slowing down the economy.

The below table indicates the debt to GDP ratio for several key countries in Europe, all of which do not appear healthy at all. This is a sign that Europe may soon follow the footsteps of the US in having to adjust its taxes. It is also one of the reasons for policy uncertainty in both US and Europe.

Country	Debt to GDP Ratio
Ireland	113%
Germany	79%
France	95%
Italy	123%
Greece	153%
Portugal	112%
Spain	80%

(Sources: World Bank, Economist magazine and IMF website)

Debts Impact on the Economy

Countries having high debt ratio walk in a precarious vicious cycle of debt trap and lower standard of living. Some challenges for the countries to confront:

1. Highly income inequality
2. Economic instability
3. Fiscal disorder—Austerity
4. Non-effective monetary policy
5. Stagnation of economy or recession.
6. High sovereign debt risk
7. High unemployment

Europe Is Dead

Europe is, technically speaking, dead. The productivity levels are low and confidence is abysmally low from global investors. As Janet Yellen winds down the Federal Reserve's money-printing operation, Mario Draghi is boosting Europe's cash supply. QE is coming to Europe. Money printing only adds poison to the economy in the form of INFLATION.

That means the dollars Yellen's Fed is removing could be compensated for by cheap euros from the European Central Bank. The result may be enough cash sloshing around to underpin this year's run-up in risk assets even if the Fed begins mulling higher interest rates too. According to the late Nobel Laureate Professor Robert Fogel, from University of Chicago, Booth School of Business, USA, in 2008: Europe's economy would become one-third of the global economy in the next 10 years. So far this has been an accurate and solid prediction. Euro currency might hit parity with US dollar by Q-3, 2015. Europe's or Euro zone GDP would be hovering around under 1% in the next 3 to 5 years creating mass unemployment and sub-par economic growth.

Japan – Abenomic Under Critical Care Unit

Japan was once among the most powerful economies of the world, but is it still so in this current era? It might not have been dominating the world economy in recent years but still did fairly well, or so it seems. Up till recently, Japan's stock market was strong and bullish but that run came to an end when it fell in 2013. Prime Minister Mr. Abe deemed that he needed to reform, given the various circumstances the country was facing. His efforts and reform campaign to turnaround the economy was known as "Abenomics". In 2013 he launched a three-part plan dubbed the "three arrows" to revive Japan's stagnant economy. His plans consist of fiscal stimulus for the country's economy, an unprecedented monetary boost through massive quantitative easing, and radical structural reforms with hopes of giving their economy a long and lasting boost which would result in sustainable growth.

Economists and historians would remember that Japan was the only thriving economy and was the world economic superpower before the Second World War. These experts would also see a similarity between Mr. Abe's current reforms and that of then-Prime Minister, Mr. Takashi. History has it that it not turn out well. Japan is also faced with an aging population and low market confidence. Tough times ahead for Japan, Europe and USA.

Topic Summary

It is clear that several of the world's leading economies are past their prime at that they are facing looming challenges. There was a time when savvy investors would put their money there but not anymore. The time has come for the rise of the East, specifically in the ASEAN region. The next topics will explore the fundamental reasons supporting this phenomenon and further zoom in on certain rapid growth areas.

Topic 2

Asia: The New Growth Story

While Western countries have had their prime, this is the time for Asia to shine. There are economic cycles whereby a region or a country goes through a growth stage, peaks, stagnant, and eventually dips. As a whole, the western countries have had their peak and some are either stagnant and some are on the verge of collapsing. Asia, on the other hand, has been experiencing steady growth and is on the verge of becoming the new global economic powerhouse. And when the market is volatile, savvy investors will choose to hold and grow their wealth in a safe and steady asset class – Real Estate.

Asia Remains Economically Resilient and Structurally Strong Amid Global Turmoil

Asia is the path of strong domestic demand and financial sound balance sheet this time around. Unlike 1997-98 Asia crisis, where currencies went down, GDP was sub-par and governments were in panic to shield their economies from speculators, this time government have done their homework and are confident to the take the heat of the market in an effective manner.

Asia will remain resilient for the next 3 to 5 years according to market intelligence reports. Asia's balance sheet is strong with capital continuously flowing into the economies. China is supporting Asia with regional investments. South Korea, Indonesia, Singapore and Malaysia are the hot bed of capital investments, consumption, strong growth trajectory and structurally healthy fiscal side. The emerging markets - Singapore, Malaysia and South Korea - have a few variables in common:

	Singapore	Malaysia	South Korea
Strong GDP	✓	✓	✓
Healthy Foreign Reserves	✓	✓	✓
Economic Confidence	✓	✓	✓
Strong Domestic Demand	✓	✓	✓
Pub/Pvt Investment	✓	✓	✓
Rising Per capita income	✓	✓	✓
Lower budget deficit	✓	✓	✓

Growing middle class	✓	✓	✓
Stable government	✓	✓	✓
Effective Monetary Policy	✓	✓	✓
Fiscal Discipline	✓	✓	✓
Current account surplus	✓	✓	✓

"Chinese Investors are Driving the Global Real Estate Boom in Asia"

China's economy has been doing well under the well-planned governance of the Chinese government. As such, there has been rise in the number of wealthy Chinese and besides living a luxurious lifestyle they have plenty of cash to spare. And in the current globalization era, such wealthy individuals invest in various assets including real estate, both locally and globally. Among the favorite investment locations for wealthy Chinese individuals include the US, UK, Australia, Dubai, and Asian countries like Malaysia and Singapore.

It is not only the Chinese but other Asian countries are also doing well economically. This wealth finds a safe haven in asset classes such as real estate. Wealthy Asians tend to be more investment focused than their European counterparts; this is another big boost to the growth of real estate, especially in Asia.

Wealthy Asians also explore and opt for a different lifestyle that is found overseas such as the US and Australia. There are migration programs which allow for easier approval when individuals or families invest or at bring over substantial amounts of wealth. This move by governments allow for huge inputs of foreign capital in either business or other investments. Many wealthy Asians transfer huge amounts of money when migrating and use that wealth to invest in real estate. This has certainly been among the factors that gave real estate a great boost.

Real Estate as the New Global Currency

Taking on from Topic 1 on the preservation of wealth and the move away from equities, real estate has emerged as a much preferred asset class. Chinese buyers are taking out their money and putting it in real estate throughout the world and with a focus on Asia. And rightfully so because real estate is tangible and cannot possibly be zero-valued, plus this is the boom of Asia. So naturally the savvy thing to do is to put one's wealth into Asian real estate.

Since the 2007 economic crisis, real estate has become the favored global currency. According to Real Capital Analytics (RCA), sales of large lot size commercial property around the world totaled over $1.1 trillion in 2013, surpassing the trillion dollar mark for the first time since 2007. Regardless of the type of real estate invested in, it is a tangible asset with scarce supply and has shown to appreciate in value over time. While US real estate has dipped in value during the last crisis and some savvy investors took the opportunity to buy under-valued real estate there, it has since appreciated in value and could possibly dip again when the US economy can no longer artificially keep afloat due to its huge debt. Stimulus packages will only cause more inflation and create a bubble waiting to burst. On the other hand, Asian real estate is appreciating in value due to fundamental factors such as the uprising economy and indeed now is the time for Asia to shine. Savvy investors know that the market has cycles and that it is now time for Asia to flourish and take its place as the leading global economy of tomorrow.

Topic Summary

It is clear that the East has come a long way and has gaining economic and financial strength. There is a shift in economic power, with ASEAN countries being very strong contenders as the next global growth area. With the West stagnated or even falling apart, Asia and specifically some ASEAN countries such as Singapore, Malaysia and South Korea are leading the pack in economic growth. While equity can be volatile and could even be zero-valued, real estate is tangible and is always in demand, especially in booming economies. Now is the time for ASEAN real estate to shine.

Malaysia: The New Safe Haven

There are economic global economic cycles as well as regional economic cycles. The savvy investor knows when and where to put his or her money for the highest returns in the shortest time. Whether it is short or long term investments, it is crucial to go into the right place at the right time. While western regions have had a good run in the past, now is the time of the Asia. Many investors are coming to Asia and ASEAN countries, and for good reason – because it is a booming region on the uptrend, with plenty of growth potential in the coming years.

Of course, investors will further zoom into the several countries in the region to determine the best options. And the key is to find countries with the right economic fundamentals, the core factors that will allow a country's economy to grow in a healthy manner. And Malaysia fits the bill just fine.

The Frontrunners of Asian Economic Growth

Countries such as Singapore and Malaysia are among the favorites while Indonesia is slowly coming up, hopefully with changes to be introduced by the new president. Brunei is stable but not so exciting for investors, and the Philippines and Vietnam need to enhance their infrastructure before they can enjoy the growth of countries like Singapore and Malaysia. Another one to look out for is Myanmar, but that will be in the next few years. So for now it will primarily be Singapore and Malaysia. In terms of real estate, do bear in mind that Singapore is relatively expansive compared to Malaysia. It has very limited land and has been exhausting the available land resources as well as reclaiming land by the sea. And even Singaporeans are starting to invest out of Singapore and into Malaysia, especially the southern region of Malaysia which is making fast progress. Just bordering Singapore and with upcoming infrastructure, Singaporeans may soon start to live in Malaysia and travel over to Singapore for work. This demand coupled with other local and foreign purchases will certainly boost the prices of Malaysian real estate.

3 Key Criteria for Strategic Investment

As real estate investors, it is crucial to consider the current economic condition and growth potential of a country before putting money in. Strong economic growth depends also on foreign direct investment (FDI) and those big players are very selective on where to enter. By understanding how they think and where they put their money, real estate investors can leverage on that boost for higher and quicker returns. It is very simple: where they pump their money will then create jobs and also spur a healthy flow of money due to the additional capital injection and also stronger spending power from the additional jobs and population drawn to that locality. Naturally, there will also be a need for residential and commercial real estate, as well as industrial land and properties for the businesses to grow. This means prices will go up!

So what do the big businesses look at before deciding to come in? Here are the three main criteria:

Cheap Energy

For businesses and production to run, large amounts of energy sources are required. It definitely makes sense to go into a place whereby there are enough of energy resources at a low cost. If the costs are high, it drives up production cost and affects compatibility or margins, whereas cheap energy means low cost of production allowing for very competitive prices. It goes beyond just the energy cost in production but also all the indirect costs such as materials (including energy used to produce the materials) and transportation. So yes, cheap energy is an important factor to consider when deciding where to build businesses.

Malaysia is among the leading energy hubs long with Singapore. Iskandar is the main driving force of Malaysia while Sabah and Sarawak (East Malaysia) has plenty of oil. Some say that Malaysia is sitting on "Black Gold". Such resources surely strengthen the country's economy and give it great potential to further grow.

Cost of Capital

In most cases, businesses put in a portion of the money and also take financing from local banks. That is the total amount of capital put into a business. The cost of capital is determined by the lending rates from local banks, often influenced by the central or national bank. Again, competitive or low costs of financing will enhance compatibility and encourage business and economic growth.

A country's interest rates are an indication of the performance of their economy and governance. There is a negative correlation between interest rates and the economy, meaning that the lower the interest rates the better the economy and vice versa. Malaysia's rates are very reasonable and this signals a strong economy. Coincidentally, there tends to be a positive correlation between interest rates and tax rates. A place like Malaysia with low interest rates has also decent tax rates, another plus point for investors.

Productive Labor Force

Hiring people to run the business is also a substantial amount of the overall business operating cost. Malaysia has a huge labor force and nearly all Malaysians speak and read English. The salaries in Malaysia are also below the average market price in the region, making it among the favorites to invest in.

The above criteria are mainly economic factors and a country's economy is largely dependent on government policies and political stability. Malaysia's positive economic factors indicate a stable government and political environment, making it a safe haven for investors.

Malaysia has strong fundamentals and the government has a solid balance sheet and has brought down budget deficit from 5-6% to 3.5% of GDP has brought financial discipline to the balance sheet. This was also highlighted in the International New York Times.

Infrastructure

Another criterion for consideration is infrastructure. This is obvious because poor infrastructure causes much inconvenience and adds on to costs of business. There must be clear distinction made between business investment and real estate investment, in terms of how established the infrastructure should be. To start a business, it needs existing good infrastructure to allow for smooth operations; to invest in real estate, there must be ample infrastructure for businesses to run but to the extent of maturity. A matured market has reached its peak while a maturing market is in the prime growth zone. A totally new market takes time and investments will be tied down for years before giving good returns. So the ideal place to invest is in one that is rapidly growing with more room to expand.

Infrastructure investment is generally seen as a major boost to the economy at the macro level because impact factor generates momentum in the economy. Its stimulates the economic growth in the form of employment, involves decision makers, supports various industries like metal, government bodies, manufacturing, technical know-how and above all its increase the productivity of labor force. Empirical evidence support that infra-structure contributes 0.3% to the GDP. The notion of the link between infrastructure investment and economic growth is supported by Nobel Laureate Professor, the late Robert Fogel from Uni of Chicago, Booth School.

Topic Summary:

ASEAN is the growth region for the upcoming years and Singapore and Malaysia are the strongest contenders of the region. Singapore has grown more rapidly than Malaysia in the past, leaving the latter with more room to grow. Singapore is already quite matured in terms of real estate and infrastructure establishment while Malaysia is on an uptrend, giving the latter much more room to grow and for real estate capital appreciation. Malaysia's natural resource of oil, lower costs of running a business and so on gives it an edge over the rest. This is the right time to invest here.

Topic 4

Three Hubs for Savvy Investors

Iskandar Malaysia is fast becoming the energy hub of the region with many companies moving in; Penang and Shah Alam are growing as manufacturing hubs; and KL is a networking hub. These areas are rapidly developing and have been receiving plenty of government and private investment, including foreign funds. It shows that these areas are doing well and we can expect further growth; it also means investing in real estate there can bring about huge gains.

Kuala Lumpur - Networking Hub

While Kuala Lumpur is the capital of Malaysia and has been developing steadily over the years, there are also other areas within the Greater KL (surroundings to the capital city) which deserve attention. We will look at Kuala Lumpur as a networking hub and also some of the savvy investment areas that should be on the radar.

Kuala Lumpur

There are several key factors to boost Kuala Lumpur (KL) as a networking hub.

The Tun Razak Exchange (TRE) – as part of Malaysia's Economic Transformation Program (ETP), the RM26 billion project, TRE, was recently launched by the prime minister. It has been seen as a positive move by economists to reshape the financial landscape of Malaysia, particularly in Islamic finance, as recently reported in InvestKL.

Conferences & Events – international events such as global or regional conferences draw visitors to a place and Kuala Lumpur is among the popular host destinations for several such conferences. For example, the third edition of Rail Business Asia, co-hosted by Land Public Transport Commission (S.P.A.D.) and Construction Industry Development Board (CIDB) Malaysia, will take place from 2 – 4 September 2015 in Kuala Lumpur Convention Centre. The Malaysian Palm Oil Board (MPOB) is co-organizing the Palm Oil Trade Fair and Seminar (POTS) 2014, which will be held in several places including Kuala Lumpur. It is expected to draw an international crowd of oils and fats industry players, marketers, traders, economists, nutritionists, government officials as well as all segments of the private industry. Kuala Lumpur also play host to other prestigious events such as Offshore Technology Conference, 2014 ASEAN Real Estate Infrastructure Summit, Islamic Banking conferences, and many other international crowd pullers. It also hosts the Formula One on an annual basis at its Sepang International Circuit which brings in huge numbers of international fans and enthusiasts. Having the right infrastructure in place such as Putra World Trade Centre (PWTC) and Kuala Lumpur Convention Centre (KLCC) along with convenient LRTs to ferry participants to such places during events and having ample hotels and accommodation near the vicinities give Kuala Lumpur an edge in playing host to international and local events. Even local events help spur the economy of Kuala Lumpur by drawing in people, creating job and business opportunities, and promoting the city's reputation.

Infrastructure and Public Transport– this is indeed an important factor to ensure that a place is easily accessible and that people will want to live there, work or do business there, or travel there when there are events or just for a holiday. Being the capital city of Malaysia, Kuala Lumpur has the best infrastructure in the country. Not only are there many highways, there are also plenty of public transportation available, such as Light Rail Transit (LRT), Monorail Line, the Commuter Train, various bus and taxi services. This encourages people to favor such a city for both business and pleasure.

High Speed Rail (HSR) – the HSR connecting Kuala Lumpur to Singapore will close the distance between the two countries and also enhance connectivity among the several areas where the HSR stops. There will be seven stops in Malaysia including: Kuala Lumpur, Putrajaya, Seremban, Ayer Keroh, Muar, Batu Pahat, and Nusajaya, reported the Straits Times. These areas will be able to easily access either or Singapore or KL and enhance both as networking hubs. In fact, all the areas surrounding the stops will benefit in terms of real estate appreciation, but Kuala Lumpur has more positive factors to boost its value and thus seems more promising than the other stops.

All these and more make Kuala Lumpur a city with plenty of activity. Would the savvy investor put money in such a place or a dead city with no activity? Definitely a place like Kuala Lumpur. And bear in mind that the prices of Kuala Lumpur real estate are still reasonably priced and relatively affordable compared to neighboring cities such as Singapore, Bangkok, Jakarta, and so on. There is still room to grow and the real estate prices will still go up.

Shah Alam

Shah Alam has a population of 750,000 and it is among the highest in the state of Selangor, the richest state in the country. It has good infrastructure and is well connected through many highways. There are award-winning townships, sports stadiums, higher learning institutions and plenty of amenities. These are all favorable factors toward the growth of Shah Alam. And there are plans for the Light Rail Transit (LRT) to be extended to Klang, passing by Shah Alam.

Another key factor for its growth is a spill-over from Klang. Klang is well known for its port and similar to Penang it is favored by manufacturer to setup facilities there due to the convenience and proximity to Port Klang. Klang's real estate are also in demand but Shah Alam is in a more strategic location causing the spill-over from Klang to Shah Alam but not the other way around. Being in between the manufacturing hub of Klang and the established and saturated townships of

Subang Jaya and Petaling Jaya, Shah Alam is among the best options for relocation from either township. Being relatively affordable in pricing than Subang Jaya and Petaling Jaya, coupled with its other favorable factors, Shah Alam looks set for growth.

Brand consciousness is also a key in determining choice of real estate purchase, especially residential property for own stay. It is a symbol of status and lifestyle which is much craved by home buyers. The iconic i-City which is also a MSC hub has boosted the brand of Shah Alam.; it is a well-planned mixed development comprising of a shopping mall, office towers, hotels, residential units and recreational parks. This was analyzed during the recent Star Property Convention, cited in The Star on 22 September 2014. It is in Shah Alam and thus it will raise the brand image of the surrounding areas and increase the real estate value. Shah Alam is among the areas that savvy investors are looking to.

Cyberjaya

Cyberjaya is part of the Greater KL in the central region of Malaysia which is fast developing and appreciating in value. People have been saying there is an oversupply of residential properties in Cyberjaya since five years back, and the current figures prove otherwise. There is an existing population of 60,000 in Cyberjaya with only 5,000 available houses, as cited in International New York Times. There is a ratio of 12 people to every one house available, which is clearly a shortage. As it is, much of the working population there are living to neighboring townships such as Puchong, Kajang, Bangi and so on and travelling to work in Cyberjaya. Some prefer it this way because Cyberjaya is still in a growing stage whereby shopping malls, eateries and entertainment outlets are just starting to come in; they choose to live in a township where these are readily available. Soon, there will be ample amenities and entertainment that it becomes convenient to live in Cyberjaya itself, plus the township is well planned with ample parking space and greenery.

Looking at this, it is clear to savvy investors that the surrounding townships have matured while Cyberjaya is upcoming. Matured townships can still enjoy further growth on a steady pace but an upcoming one will see much more rapid capital appreciation in a short period of time. And to make things more interesting, there are other factors that will boost the value of Cyberjaya real estate.

There are existing universities and upcoming ones in Cyberjaya; this will certainly provide a strong student demand for housing within the vicinity. The government has shifted its administrative centre to Putrajaya, just beside Cyberjaya, and there will be thousands of civil servants needing homes. KLIA2, the second international airport of Malaysia has just started operations and it is very near to Cyberjaya; airline staff needs accommodation and some foreigners also favor living in a place near the airport. All these factors and more will further boost Cyberjaya's real estate demand and boost its value. Also remember that this development is back by the government and following the big players will not go wrong.

Penang - Manufacturing Hub

Due to its strategic location near the sea and with ports available for import and export, Penang is favored as one of the manufacturing hubs of not only Malaysia but also for the ASEAN region. Malaysia, having the right factors as mentioned in Topic 3, and Penang, being in a strategic location with the right infrastructure, makes it a clear choice for mega corporations to setup manufacturing facilities in this location. Many large corporations, especially the Japanese, have long been present in the island of Penang. And lately it has received further good news of more investments coming its way.

As reported in The Star on 9 June 2014, SanDisk Corporation, listed in NASDAQ and is also a Fortune 500 and S&P 500 company, is putting up a RM1.2 billion manufacturing plant over a 30 acre site in Penang and is expected to recruit over 1,000 employees; the plant is scheduled to start production in March 2015. This will future spur the growth of Penang as it creates more jobs and increases the local spending power and also indirectly stimulate the economy and increase GDP. Areas near any site such as this will also benefit from the economies generated around it and real estate would appreciate in value.

To add to the good news, Penang Chief Minister Lim Guan Eng announced that an American multinational firm, Seagate, which are already present in Penang will further invest an additional RM1.05 billion to expand its operations, possibly buying up an additional 40 to 70 acres of land to fulfill the necessary capacity, reported the Malaysia Insider on 9 August 2014. This comes to show that Penang is indeed a strategic place for manufacturing and that it is a successful one too. More of such investments can be expected and the state of Penang will surely flourish.

On top of being a manufacturing hub, Penang is also a tourist attraction to both local and foreign tourists. Penang has some historic sites as well as plenty of good food. While this may not spur the economy as much as the manufacturing industry does, it is no doubt an additional bonus that creates many jobs and business opportunities. The second Penang Bridge is also up and running, making transportation smoother and easier. Real estate prices have been on the rise and are expected to keep on the uptrend.

Iskandar - Energy Hub

The growth of Iskandar has been getting a lot of attention and many have put their money there. It has come to a point where some people are questioning the number of luxury properties built there and if there is an oversupply. The answer to this is straightforward: there is ample demand take up the units built. The Japanese, Koreans, and Singaporeans are coming to Iskandar and soon there will be international schools and universities. As the population grows there will be plenty of demand to take up all the available units.

Just like the manufacturing hub in Penang, being the energy hub will draw in local and foreign investment and create job and business opportunities. As reported in IskandarMalaysia. com, Iskandar is fast becoming the leading energy hub of the region due to its strategic location in the oil trading route and because it is conducive to serve the needs of the oil and gas industry; there it is near to some of Malaysia's oil reserves. It is the centre for several related activities including oil refinery, storage and regasification plants, petrochemical refineries, oil storage, petroleum support service hub and other related activities. There is a growing demand for storage, refinery and petrochemical businesses in the region and Iskandar is ideal because of its strategic location, vast availability of land resources, deep waters, and it has an edge over Singapore because there is more available land. Infrastructure is well established and this growth is also backed by the government in terms of putting in place several initiatives under the Economic Transformation Program (ETP) to make it a success. Besides being blessed with natural resources and being a strategic location with government support, Iskandar is also the centre for building up renewable energy and solar power capacity. This national project is too big to fail and the direct and indirect effects of it will be very positive outcomes. There will be funds coming in, more economic activity and growth, more demand for housing and other businesses, which will have a snowball effect of the booming of Iskandar. As foreign businesses begin to take advantage of this opportunity and take a position here, there will be further need for international school and other amenities, making Iskandar a truly booming place with lots of investment opportunities for the savvy investor.

And the fact that it is neighboring Singapore gives it a huge advantage because of the difference in real estate pricing. It should be no surprise that the prices in Iskandar are relatively affordable compared to Singapore and that Singaporeans would find it attractive to invest or even to stay in Iskandar. At present, some people do not mind living in Iskandar or nearby places and travelling to Singapore on a daily basis to work. It may not be the most convenient option but the work costs saving of living in Iskandar make it feasible enough for some to take this option. And once the High Speed Train is ready it will become an even more popular choice. There will be spillovers from Singapore, further driving up the demand for housing in Iskandar.

Topic Summary

Malaysia as a whole is a good place to invest in and there are some key areas that deserve more attention than others. The key is to look at the economic activities in a place and evaluate if there is substantial investment and development there to drive up a real demand for real estate. The hubs discussed above fit the bill because of the massive resources put in either through government or private funds that stimulate the growth of those areas. Once a place has the right infrastructure and is getting plenty if funds pouring in, there will be plenty of activity and people will need a place to stay. This is far from mere speculation because there is an actual need to house all those people. And when demand increases, so does the price of real estate.

Follow The Big Players

As we narrow down from region to country to zones and so on, there is still the final decision of choosing the exact areas to invest in. One good strategy is to go with the big players because their investments into a specific area will surely spur its growth. Such areas are definitely a good bet because the big players will see it through and investors who ride along with it will reap the benefits from the efforts of the big players. That is savvy investing!

High Speed Rail

The Malaysia and Singapore governments are working together to connect the two countries via a high speed train. The train will connect Kuala Lumpur and Singapore, figuratively closing the distance between the two countries. And since Singapore's estate prices are much higher, there will be a spillover of Singaporeans who choose to live in the currently more affordable Malaysia. With such demands, investors will also put their money along the railway especially near the stations. The prices of real estate will surely surge. And what does the savvy investor do? Join in the ride, of course!

Both countries will benefit from this infrastructure, but more so Malaysia because the 90 minute ride consists of over an hour in Malaysia and only a short duration in Singapore. This means more development and growth as well as job opportunities in Malaysia. In April 2014, the Prime Ministers of both countries have agreed that the final station in Kuala Lumpur will be in Sungai Besi. So places around Sungai Besi, Cheras, and Bandar Tasik Selatan which are close to the train station in will greatly benefit from the high speed train. On top of that there will be job opportunities around those areas, such as employment for the train station and high speed train, and indirectly from other development in that vicinity. These employees need a place to stay and it drives up demand and prices of real estate.

Sovereign Wealth Funds (SWFs)

The savvy investor knows that such funds are state reserves that are put to invest in long term initiatives. This simply means that the government is pumping money into certain areas and that they tend to have at least a 15 to 20 year effort to build that area before moving on once the job is done. There are several prominent SWFs to take note of, from and beyond Malaysia. Some good examples include Khazanah of Malaysia, CIC of China, Temasik of Singapore, Idea UAE, Kuwait Investment Authority, Qatar Investment Authority and Saudi Sovereign Fund. These funds take long term positions in a development and it is worthwhile to keep track of their investments by keeping updated through newspapers or the internet.

And for this reason, Topic 4 suggests to focus on some of the major hubs in Malaysia. With such funds coming in to grow an area, it looks certain that growth will take place in the next few years. When the government is behind the project, rest assured the infrastructure will be well in place. The key takeaway is to follow and invest in areas backed by the government.

Universities

One university can sometimes be enough to create a population large enough to form a township, what more an area with several universities. Seldom in Malaysia do we see a whole are with nothing but universities; usually there are residential and commercial areas around it. And this is great because there is ample opportunity for the savvy investor to buy real estate in those areas surrounding the universities.

Typically a newly opened university can conservatively expect to draw in 1,000 to 2,000 students in the initial stages. It could soon grow to over 5,000 or more in a short time. While some universities do provide hostel accommodation for students, there is still ample demand for accommodation in the surrounding areas. Commercial properties will also be in demand as there is a growing population which creates business opportunities. Whether it is an area with existing universities or upcoming ones, the demand and the prices of real estate look very optimistic.

Among the reasons for the boom of education and universities in Malaysia include the country's political, economical, financial, and infrastructure stability. These factors are important for investors and students because without such stability there is no guarantee of sustainability in their investments or education here; Malaysia has been constantly giving such confidence globally. Not only does it have an assurance for all who come in, it also provides much convenience and flexibility by having good infrastructure including public transport systems which is a good alternative for those who do not drive or choose not to drive into prime areas during peak hours. And with a huge English-speaking population, Malaysia is indeed a friendly place for foreign students.

Topic Summary

It is very simple, just follow the big players such as government backed projects, SWFs, and universities. Such powerful forces will ensure the success and growth of an area and thus bring up the demand and prices of real estate there. Keep informed of the moves of these big players and put your money where they put their. They will push the growth and the savvy investors get to enjoy the momentum and profits!

Future Outlook of Malaysia

- Leading economy of the ASEAN Bloc

Many of the good investment regions are past their prime while some upcoming ones are not making the cut just yet. Europe is very much dead in terms of its economy; Japan is currently struggling; Africa is having issues with ebola; South America has yet to find its growth direction. Asia is the place to be for economic growth and Malaysia is among the prime candidates is Asia and ASEAN.

Market Confidence

Malaysia has a good combination of all factors as covered in earlier topics. It also has a growing population which will add to the productive working force and gross domestic produce (GDP). More people also means more spending, which will stimulate the economy. And not only is the overall population growing, so is the middle class. There are now more middle class residents in Malaysia then there ever was before and this means more spending power. This middle class population has more money at hand and they tend to save more, invest more, and consume more. All these are healthy for the country's growth and a positive sign of the country's stability.

Ultimately it is about market confidence. Without it, people would be uncertain of the future and tend to keep resources on standby. This means less investment and consumption, causing ripple effects on slowing down the economy. But this is certainly not the case in Malaysia. On the contrary, Malaysia's steady growth over the years has given confidence to locals as well as foreigners. Locals are willing to spend on consumption and to invest, stimulating the economy, while investors from abroad are confident to put their money here. And with the slowdown of other countries past their prime or upcoming countries still struggling to get their act together, it leaves Malaysia as a prime candidate for foreign direct investments (FDI) and other forms of investment including real estate. Coupled with its own natural resources and healthy governance and economy, Malaysia is set for growth in the upcoming years.

And since real estate is the new global currency, what better way to keep and grow your wealth than in Malaysian real estate. Real estate is the way to go and Malaysia is the place to be right now.

Ringgit to Stay Resilient Despite Exogenous / Unpredictable Factors Globally

At present, Malaysian government has demonstrated some remarkable fiscal brinkmanship in containing the budget deficit 3.5 % of GDP. This resulted in boosting economic growth [GDP over 6%] and consolidation of the balance sheet. With confidence in the economy running high from local and private investors, solid FDI $13 billion, healthy foreign exchange reserves of $138 billion roughly, unemployment at 3%, the Ringgit will remain resilient in context to global exogenous factors like questionable recovery numbers in USA/European financial crisis and policy failure [Abenomics] in Japan to be around parity of RM 3.30 to 3.43 against dollar by 2015. GDP size is expected to touch $332 billion by 2015 up from $248 billion in 2008. Structured GDP rate would be trading between 5% and 5.3% in 2015. Macro fundamentals are pretty solid and outlook remains positive / stable. Malaysia is a five star country moving into seven star league.

No Financial Crisis Looming

As much as some people think there is a financial crisis looming, we have to look at the fundamentals of Malaysia before jumping to any conclusion. While western countries are slowing down, ASEAN and especially Malaysia is picking up. The Malaysian GDP is on an upsurge, foreign reserves are high at USD$140billion and there is political stability. There is strong domestic support from both public and private sectors and GDP growths of 4.8% to 5.2% are expected. The central bank of Malaysia also reported a healthy household debt with 47.1% being purchase of residential property and 20% for the purchase of motor vehicles.

The local government is well prepared and is taking strategic measure to help Malaysians be more independent and financially savvy. The gradual decrease of subsidies and so on will get locals geared up for any financial implications from the west. By easing into realistic pricing without government subsidies, it leaves the government more room to focus on the nation's growth and development.

GDP consists of consumption, investment, government and export. Malaysia's GDP has been rising and will continue to rise because the factors are all well in place. Consumption patterns, domestic demand and aggregate demand are strong as well as investments coming from both government and private sectors. Private sectors create the bulk of the job opportunities, giving the people ample resources (money) to stimulate the economy and GDP; the government provides a safe environment for this t happen, giving everyone the confidence to produce and to spend.

Real Estate Prices on a Steady Rise

During the global financial crisis in 2007-2008, Malaysian real estate was not hard hit like some of the other countries. No doubt there was a slowdown in the local market, but it quickly rebound and prices went up to levels higher than before yet still very reasonable compared to cities in the region. This means the prices are still very reasonable and has room to grow. Among the factors pushing up prices are strong local demand and large amounts of foreign investment. The fact that foreign investors choose not to invest in their homelands but to invest here indicates a discrepancy in pricing as well as potential room for growth. Why else would they come all the way here and put in large amounts of money? Prices have been on the rise for the past few years and have been continuing to go up in spite of anything that some people are saying. Some mistakenly thought that the rapid growth of Malaysian real estate was leading to artificially high prices and ultimately a bubble burst. But in fact it was merely the case of catching up with the country's economic growth and also with the regional prices. It is still on the uptrend and in the midst to catching up, with plenty of room to grow!

Bubble Burst? What Bubble?

There have been concerns that the prices in Kuala Lumpur have been rising too much and might crash, like in the case of Dubai. Having understood the fundamentals of this growth and also the difference between a bull run and a bubble, we know this will not happen. Another key factor to take note of is the percentage of ownership of the properties. In Dubai, about 80% of the real estate were held by foreign investors while it is the opposite in Kuala Lumpur; 80% of the real estate are owned by locals; this was cited in International new York Times, 10 October 2014. This is important because an area overly dependent on foreign investment indicates a lack of local demand and consumption, a lack of fundamental support for growth. So having high local ownership shows that Kuala Lumpur has the right fundamentals and that the growth is based on true confidence in the local scenario with strong economic stability.

Compared to other countries in the region, Kuala Lumpur and Malaysia real estate is still very affordable. It would not be surprising if certain real estate in Malaysia appreciate in value by another 50% or more in the next few years, especially in areas where there is upcoming infrastructure such as MRTs and the High Speed Rail.

Local Real Estate Trends

Some locals may complain that the prices of affordable housing are too high; this is very relative. Compared to other cities in neighboring countries, it is rather reasonable here. The reason there is a sentiment of high prices is because locals have been pampered by government subsidies and control of pricing that when real estate prices went up due to natural market movements, they were not mentally ready to accept it. In fact, there are plenty of housing available in Malaysia, perhaps just not as near to the town centre as some hoped for. Land is limited and as there is hardly any available land left in the city centre, developers are trying to maximize the usage of available land by building high rise buildings such as apartments and condominiums. These are conveniently located with plenty of amenities and facilities but come at smaller sizes compared to landed properties. Dreaming of a landed home in the city centre might be a bit of a stretch for some people, and they could opt for a high rise home or to opt for a landed home slightly further away. And with new infrastructure such as MRTs and highways coming up, it closes the distance between those "far away" locations and the town centre. What may have needed an hour to reach before a new highway is ready could now only require 20 minutes. Many people are opting to live slightly further out in order to enjoy a spacious home with greenery around, and yet be able to travel a quick distance to work at the busy cities. People are starting to accept the reality of the market forces and are making the best of it; some have made huge profits by investing in a savvy manner, following the right trends.

Due to the congestion in city centers, developers are starting to the outskirts too. Many have acquired land banks in the outskirts and were waiting for the right time to start their huge development plans there. As infrastructure is falling in place, this would be the right time to start developing the outskirts. Savvy investors know that the prices of a relatively new outskirt development are currently at the lower spectrum and can only go in one direction – upwards! This is a great opportunity to enter at the early stages and enjoy the uptrend ride.

Bubble vs. Bull Run

Rapidly increasing prices of real estate could be either the start of a bubble or of a bull run. Both look very optimistic at a superficial level but there is a huge underlying difference: the fundamentals of the economy. When prices are surging without a strong economic foundation, there will come a time in the near future that it all falls apart when people realize that those real estate are overpriced and have gone way ahead of the economic growth; it will be the case of an inflation and the government's best tool to control it would be to increase interest rates. This will hamper FDI and business growth, amongst other things, and result in an economic downturn. This sudden realization could cause real estate price to fall and investors who were blindly buying would be burnt. The increased interest rates would also cause many investors to lose holding power and be forced into letting go of their real estate in the quickest time possible, at any price! This is a bubble burst.

A bull run, on the other hand, is caused by public confidence and for good reason. With strong economic fundamental such as stability, conducive business and investment environment and FDI pouring in, there is massive growth and a real demand for real estate to accommodate to the development. Such a bull run could slow down after its span of growth but the economy could still be stable and real estate prices would remain on an uptrend despite at a slower rate. Savvy investors would have made a great deal of profit during the bull run and can choose to continue holding on to their real estate of to take position in the next booming place to enjoy another bull run.

The key is this: a Bubble is when there is an illusion of confidence and growth which is in fact not sustainable; a Bull Run is when there is actual growth with all the fundamentals in place to sustain it, confidence and price increase are merely natural outcomes of the bullish circumstances.

A country with Five Star Stability

Malaysia has all the fundamentals right and can be said to have five star stability. It is very stable in the five key areas that provide the basis of a strong and growing economy, and thus the five stars.

Political Stability

The Malaysian political scenario is healthy with a long-time and stable government. No doubt that the opposition party is trying to beat the ruling party in every general election, but this is normal in any political scenario anywhere in the world. The ruling party has been in power since 1957 and the opposition party has been gaining some ground in recent elections. This is a positive and healthy situation whereby there is no absolute power by either party and that both sides will do their best to take care of the people's and country's interest. There is healthy check and balance in Malaysia's political scenario and it does not matter who wins the next general elections because either one will still be under the close watch of the other and will have to do things right.

Economic Stability

The economic growth of Malaysia has been consistent over the years and is doing well with an expected GDP growth of between 4.8% to 5.2%. Interest rates are relatively low, indicating a healthy economy. Property prices are also very reasonable and remained relatively stable through the 2007 global economic crisis; this shows that prices are not over inflated and thus did not crash during the crisis. And with political stability and the government making good efforts to build infrastructure, the economy will receive a further boost from both local and foreign investments.

Financial Stability

The government has been keeping healthy balance sheets and the GDP is good; some people cautioned of "high debt" but they probably missed out the finer details indicating that the majority of Malaysian debt is derived from real estate financing. This is a healthy sign as compared to high credit card debt or other in liabilities rather than appreciating assets, such as real estate. We also have to consider the fact that the ratio of debt to non-performing loans (NPLs) is relatively low at only xx%. Overall the Malaysian financial situation is stable and healthy.

Infrastructure Stability

Malaysia is well connected through major roads and highways and has been improving its infrastructure over the years. There are also public transportation systems such as trains and the light rail transit (LRT) with further expansion works currently in progress. This will bring about great convenience to those having to travel to busy areas such as the city centre, or from the city centre to other areas within the Greater KL region. The second Penang Bridge is complete and the high speed rail will be ready in the near future. Malaysia is steadily improving its infrastructure; it is already reasonably well established and has attracted foreign investment due to the convenience and accessibility provided. With more infrastructure put in place, it will certainly attract more investors, boosting the economy, as well as boost increase the value of real estate in places that directly or indirectly benefit from the convenience of the infrastructure.

Lifestyle Stability

People living in Malaysia know that the lifestyle is very predictable, and in a positive way. There is ample entertainment and plenty of good food available, with local food being one of the major attractions to foreign tourists; even locals love the food here and never get bored of it. While this may seem nice, how is it relevant to the country's well being? The fact is Malaysia is a very lovely place to be and there have been plenty of tourists visiting every year. In 2013, there were 25.72 million of tourists to Malaysia and the figures have been on a steady rise over the years, as cited by Tourism Malaysia. This not only boosts the economy but is also a clear indicator that it is a nice place to be. And there is a migration program known as Malaysia My Second Home (MM2H) which provides a 10 year visa and unlimited stay during the tenure to foreigners taking up the program. There have been many takers including people from Asia as well as European and other parts of the world. Besides the above attractions, Malaysia is also blessed with stable weather and "summer all year long" which many foreigners love; it is also good for manufacturing as the stable weather allows for steady production without having to cater to different seasons and weathers. Not only is Malaysia stable and very livable, it is a very nice place to live in. This means more people coming over and more money coming in.

Foreign Direct Investment (FDI)

Transportation and technology has made the world well connected and businesses are free to go where the best potential is. After all it is a free market. In the 19th century, London was the place to be; in the 20th century it was New York; now in the 21st century it is Asia's turn to excel with rapid growth. This will be the growth story for the next five to 10 years with many companies relocating to Asia and especially Malaysia. Iskandar Malaysia is fast becoming the oil and gas hub of the region with many companies moving in; Penang and Shah Alam are growing as manufacturing hubs; and KL is a networking hub. Foreign funds have been flowing in because of the stability in Malaysia.

The guideline as mentioned in Topic 5 is to follow the big players as they would certainly do thorough deal diligence before putting in such large amounts of money and taking on a long term position. So we can be very sure that a country pouring in with FDI is doing well and that investments in such a country are safe. On top of that a country's economy will also be greatly boosted by the development brought about by such investments. So not only will real estate investment in such a country be safe, it can expect great capital appreciation in the near future. The trick is to take position in the booming economy, not the ones past their prime or the ones still needing more infrastructure or stability to start enjoying rapid growth. Savvy investors want to be in the prime growth zone (right time, right place) for the largest and fastest returns.

What the Government is Doing

ASEAN economy needs infra-structure investment amounting to $1000 billion to spur growth to have sustainable economic trajectory for the next 15 to 20 years.

Infrastructure investment and economic growth has positive correlation in keeping the momentum in the economy. Malaysian PM Najib Razak and Indonesian President Jokowi are both focusing on this strategy to spur growth rate for the next 5 to 10 years. The late Nobel Laureate Professor Robert Fogel from University of Chicago Booth School of Business wrote a paper in 1964 about Japanese high speed train Shinkansen. Solid argument from the prof. News from Wall Street.

Goods & Services Tax (GST)

Effective April 2015, Malaysia implemented GST at a rate of 6%. Except for a few categories of goods and services exempted from GST, almost all others will be affected. This would increase the cost of production and in turn bring up the final price to consumers. 6% is not a lot and the Malaysian market should have no problem adapting to it. A few cents more for a meal or a drink would not be felt by the majority of the population; but big ticket items would see a more significant increase in price.

For real estate, the cost of raw materials and services rendered by professionals and sub-contractors would incur GST. Residential real estate will not be subject to GST at the final phase of transaction to consumers, while commercial real estate would be. This means both would incur higher cost to build and commercial real estate would also be taxed at the transaction point, making the increase even more significant. Residential real estate is expected to increase by about 3% due to the cost of construction, and commercial by 6% due to cost of construction and transaction. Taking a 1 million Ringgit property and adding an extra 3% or 6% brings the difference to 30,000 or 60,000, a substantial difference to homebuyers and an attractive profit to investors.

As shared by Shan Saeed in the International New York Times on 7 November 2014, the implementation of GST would increase the prices of primary and secondary market properties but would not deter people from buying, including foreign investors. Investors might take the opportunity to buy before April 2015, and even after the price increase people would continue to buy. After all, it is a solid asset class and it is also a necessity. Plus, it is on the uptrend.

Topic Summary

Malaysia has strong economic fundamentals and that is the driving force behind the growth of the nation and the country's real estate. There are economic cycles and this time it is in Malaysia that rapid growth is taking place. All factors indicate further growth for Malaysia in the upcoming years and real estate has proven to be the fastest growing asset class in

Malaysia. So it would be clear to the savvy investor that the right time, right place, and right asset class is Malaysian real estate, now! The big players are in, just follow them and reap the rewards.

AFTERWORD

With the shift in economic power towards Asia and with Malaysia's potential growth at the current moment, it is ideal to be investing here right now. And what better asset class to choose than one that is tangible and can provide healthy gains. Although we can expect general growth of the Malaysian real estate prices, there are specific areas that could give higher and faster returns. Savvy investors understand the fundamentals in analyzing an area. Big players also look at the fundamentals before putting in huge sums of money and so it is wise to follow their footsteps. For one, they already did the homework for you; secondly, they are putting in huge investments that will further spur growth.

It is the sincere hope of the authors that our readers will be able to gain some insights into the global and regional economic changes, as well as understand the great potential of real estate in Malaysia and the simple yet powerful strategies to apply. More importantly, we hope you will take action to protect and to grow your wealth in Malaysian real estate, like how savvy investors would.

ABOUT IQI HOLDINGS

IQI GROUP
International Quality Investments

Who We Are

At IQI we believe in doing things differently. We are an international property and investment company with headquarters in Kuala Lumpur, Malaysia and offices in KL, Penang, Dubai and Singapore. We work in many diverse sectors including: investments, venture capital investments, property sales, rentals, marketing, project evaluations and international sales.

Founded in 2011 we have quickly established a reputation for excellence, offering cutting edge business, retail and investment services worldwide. We have done this by bringing together some of the industry's best minds and expertise from across the world. In this short period of time we have grown exponentially and boast $120M of international property sales. This is complemented with an impressive market reach bolstered by links to institutional investors and access to over 300 dedicated sales staff in Malaysia alone.

What Makes Us Different

We embrace change and are constantly challenging tradition because we have a strong desire to improve the way our industry operates. We do business differently to give our clients the edge.

Our innovative approach takes commercial investment methodologies and uses them for our retail customers. This means our choice of properties and investments are always analysed to ensure the best possible yields. In this way we create a tailored service for the clients we serve.

Locally Sensitive Operations

We operate internationally in Malaysia, Singapore, Hong Kong, United Kingdom, United States and Dubai. While global operations can create complexities, when running our global operations we take the time to understand our surroundings and provide locally sensitive services. This ensures our clients get the best possible entry into markets.

Our Values

We believe in providing excellence in everything we do. From our business services to our real estate investments we Dare to Dream Big. What lies at the heart of our company however, is our spirit of honesty and integrity. We believe that without this foundation we would not be able to deliver outstanding services for our clients.

Investing In People

We invest in people and support entrepreneurship. Through our investment services we help entrepreneurs gain access to the capital they need to achieve their goals. It is not just capital investments that we provide, but also the vital support and expertise that can help guide young businesses to success.

Giving Back

We enrich lives not only with our capital investments but by giving to various charitable causes. Giving back to the community is important in fulfilling our corporate and social responsibilities. One such example is our active support of the Rumah Aman orphanage in Malaysia. We believe by giving back to projects like these and for others around the world, we are making a wise investment for our future.

IQI Website: www.iqi-group.com